YOUTUBE MONETIZATION SIMPLIFIED

"Unlocking Profit: Demystifying YouTube Monetization"

VINCENT SIMS

Copyright ©

Dedication

"To all aspiring content creators navigating the digital landscape, may this book serve as your compass on the journey to financial empowerment through YouTube. Your dedication and passion fuel the digital era, and this guide is dedicated to helping you simplify the path to successful monetization. Keep creating, keep thriving."

Table of Contents

Acknowledgments

"I extend my deepest gratitude to the vibrant community of content creators whose dedication and innovation continue to shape the digital realm. Special thanks to those who generously shared their insights and experiences, enriching the pages of this book. My appreciation also goes to friends, family, and mentors whose support and encouragement made this endeavor possible. Together, we unravel the intricacies of YouTube monetization, simplifying the journey for creators worldwide."

Preface

"In the ever-evolving landscape of digital content creation, navigating the complexities of YouTube monetization can be both thrilling and challenging. This book, 'YouTube Monetization Simplified,' emerges as a compass for creators seeking financial success in the expansive world of online videos.

As the platform transforms, so do the strategies for thriving within it. In this preface, we set the stage for a comprehensive journey, breaking down the intricacies of YouTube's monetization features. From understanding ad revenue to unlocking alternative income streams, this guide is designed to simplify the process, providing both novice and seasoned creators with actionable insights.

Embrace this resource as a roadmap, offering practical tips, case studies, and a holistic perspective on the art and science of YouTube monetization. Whether you're a budding creator with a dream or an established channel looking to refine your strategy, this book aims to empower you with the knowledge needed to thrive in the dynamic world of online content.

As we embark on this exploration together, may 'YouTube Monetization Simplified' be a valuable companion, illuminating the path to financial success and creative fulfillment. Let the journey begin!"

Chapter 1

Introduction to YouTube Monetization

- Understanding the Basics

In the vast landscape of online content creation, YouTube stands as a powerhouse, providing a platform for creators to share their creativity with a global audience. Beyond its role as a canvas for expression, YouTube also offers the enticing prospect of monetization, allowing creators to turn their passion into a sustainable source of income.

Unlocking the Monetization Gateway

YouTube Monetization is essentially the process through which content creators earn revenue from their videos. While the allure of financial reward is clear, understanding the fundamentals is crucial to navigating this realm effectively.

1. Eligibility Criteria: The Starting Line

Before delving into the intricacies of YouTube Monetization, creators must meet certain eligibility criteria. Typically, this involves adhering to YouTube's Partner Program policies, which may include having a minimum number of subscribers and watch hours over the past 12 months.

2. Ad Revenue: The Cornerstone

Ad revenue is at the core of YouTube Monetization. When ads are displayed on your videos, you earn a share of the revenue generated. This model encourages creators to produce engaging, high-quality content that attracts advertisers and keeps viewers coming back for more.

3. Ad Formats: Diversifying Income Streams

YouTube offers various ad formats, from skippable ads to non-skippable ads, bumper ads, and more. Each format presents creators with unique opportunities to optimize their revenue streams. Understanding these formats empowers creators to tailor their content to maximize earnings.

4. Viewer Engagement: The X-Factor

Beyond the numbers, viewer engagement plays a pivotal role. YouTube values not just the quantity but the quality of interaction. High viewer engagement, measured by likes, comments, and shares, not only enhances the visibility of your content but also contributes to increased ad revenue.

5. Alternative Monetization Streams: Beyond Ads

While ad revenue is a significant contributor, diversifying income streams adds stability. This includes exploring memberships, channel subscriptions, merchandise shelves, and other features that YouTube offers to creators looking to enhance their financial sustainability.

In this introductory exploration of YouTube Monetization, we've laid the groundwork for understanding the basics. From eligibility criteria to ad revenue and alternative income streams, creators embarking on the monetization journey should view this knowledge as a foundation for building a successful and rewarding presence on YouTube.

As we delve deeper into each facet of YouTube Monetization, this guide aims to demystify the process, providing practical insights and actionable strategies. Whether you're an aspiring creator or a seasoned professional, the journey to monetization begins with a solid grasp of these fundamental principles. So, let's navigate the exciting terrain of YouTube Monetization together, unlocking the potential for financial success and creative fulfillment.

- Eligibility Requirements

Before creators can start capitalizing on their content through YouTube Monetization, they must successfully clear the eligibility hurdles set by the platform. These criteria serve as a gateway, ensuring that only committed and quality content creators can participate in the revenue-sharing opportunities provided by YouTube.

1. Channel Eligibility: The Starting Point

To be eligible for YouTube Monetization, your channel must meet some foundational requirements:

- Follow YouTube Policies: Your channel must adhere to YouTube's Community Guidelines, Terms of Service, and Copyright rules. Any violations may disqualify your channel from monetization eligibility.

- Geographical Availability: Check whether YouTube Monetization is available in your region. Not all countries have the same eligibility criteria due to regional variations in advertising policies.

2. Subscriber Milestone: Building an Audience

YouTube emphasizes the importance of building an engaged audience. Creators need to have at least 1,000 subscribers on their channel before they can apply for monetization. This milestone reflects a level of commitment and community building that aligns with YouTube's vision for monetization.

3. Watch Hours Requirement: Showcasing Engagement

In addition to subscribers, YouTube expects channels to have accumulated 4,000 watch hours over the past 12 months. This metric gauges viewer engagement and demonstrates that your content resonates with a substantial audience.

4. Join the YouTube Partner Program: The Monetization Gateway

To enable monetization on your channel, you must join the YouTube Partner Program (YPP). This program consolidates various monetization features and provides a unified platform for creators to access revenue streams.

5. AdSense Account: Financial Gateway

To receive payments from YouTube, creators need an AdSense account linked to their YouTube channel. This account handles the financial aspects of monetization, ensuring creators get compensated for their content.

Navigating YouTube Monetization eligibility requirements is an essential step in the journey toward turning passion into profit. By meeting these criteria, creators not only gain access to ad revenue but also signal their commitment to producing high-quality, engaging content.

Aspiring content creators should view these requirements not as hurdles but as benchmarks that reflect the commitment and resonance of their work with the YouTube community. Embracing these eligibility criteria positions creators for success, setting the stage for a rewarding journey in the dynamic world of online content creation.

- Setting Up Your Channel for Monetization

Embarking on the journey of YouTube Monetization involves more than just meeting eligibility requirements; it requires a strategic approach to optimize your channel for revenue generation. Here's a guide on setting up your channel for monetization success:

1. Content Quality and Consistency: The Foundation

- Create Compelling Content: Consistently produce high-quality, engaging content that resonates with your target audience. Quality content not only attracts viewers but also keeps them coming back.

- Stick to a Schedule: Regular uploads help build anticipation and loyalty among your audience. Establish a content schedule that aligns with your production capabilities and audience preferences.

2. Optimize Metadata: Boosting Discoverability

- Keyword-rich Titles: Craft titles that not only capture attention but also incorporate relevant keywords related to your content. This enhances your video's discoverability in search results.

- Engaging Thumbnails: Design eye-catching thumbnails that accurately represent your video content. Thumbnails are often the first impression your video makes, influencing click-through rates.

- Detailed Descriptions and Tags: Provide detailed video descriptions with relevant keywords. Use tags strategically to improve your video's visibility within YouTube's search and recommendation algorithms.

3. Viewer Engagement: Cultivating a Community

- Encourage Interaction: Prompt viewers to like, comment, and share your videos. Increased engagement not only enhances the visibility of your content but also contributes to higher ad revenue.

- Respond to Comments: Foster a sense of community by engaging with your audience through comments. Responding to comments encourages viewer interaction and strengthens your connection with your audience.

4. Playlists and Series: Enhancing Watch Time

- Create Playlists: Organize your videos into playlists to encourage longer viewing sessions. Playlists keep viewers engaged, contributing to higher watch time, a crucial metric for monetization.

- Develop Series: Consider creating series or themed content that encourages viewers to watch multiple videos in a single sitting. This helps boost overall watch time on your channel.

5. Promotion and Collaboration: Broadening Your Reach

- Promote on Social Media: Share your videos across social media platforms to reach a broader audience. Increased visibility can lead to more subscribers and higher watch hours.

- Collaborate with Others: Collaborate with other YouTubers in your niche.

Cross-promotion exposes your channel to new audiences and can accelerate your subscriber growth.

Setting up your channel for monetization success requires a multifaceted approach that goes beyond meeting the basic eligibility criteria. By focusing on content quality, optimizing metadata, cultivating viewer engagement, and strategically promoting your channel, you lay the groundwork for a thriving YouTube presence.

Remember, YouTube Monetization is not just about earning revenue; it's about building a sustainable and rewarding relationship with your audience. As you implement these strategies, keep your creative passion at the forefront, and watch your channel evolve into a monetization success story.

Chapter 2.

Creating Quality Content for Monetization

- Identifying Marketable Niches

Quality content is the cornerstone of successful YouTube monetization. While meeting eligibility criteria is essential, the heart of the matter lies in producing videos that captivate your audience and keep them coming back for more. Here's a guide on creating content that not only meets YouTube's standards but also positions you within lucrative and marketable niches.

1. Know Your Audience: Tailor Content to Viewer Interests

- Audience Research: Understand the demographics, interests, and preferences of your target audience. Craft content that resonates with them, addressing their needs, questions, or entertainment preferences.

- Analytics Insights: Utilize YouTube Analytics to gain insights into viewer behavior. Identify popular videos, viewer demographics, and watch time patterns. This data helps refine your content strategy.

2. Trend Analysis: Stay Current and Relevant

- Stay Informed: Keep an eye on industry trends, current events, and emerging topics. Creating content around trending subjects can attract more viewers as people actively search for relevant content.

- Google Trends: Use tools like Google Trends to identify rising search queries. Aligning your content with these trends increases the likelihood of your videos being discovered by a broader audience.

3. Explore Untapped Niches: Balance Demand and Competition

- Niche Selection: Identify niches with a balance of demand and manageable competition. While popular topics attract more viewers, niches with less competition provide opportunities for quicker growth.

- Sub-Niche Exploration: Dive deeper into broader niches to discover sub-niches. This allows you to cater to specific interests within a larger category, potentially attracting a more dedicated audience.

4. Consistency and Branding: Build a Recognizable Identity

- Consistent Style: Maintain a consistent style across your videos. This includes visual elements, tone, and overall branding. Consistency helps build a recognizable identity for your channel.

- Unique Selling Proposition (USP):** Define what sets your content apart. Whether it's a unique perspective, approach, or delivery, having a USP makes your channel memorable and distinctive.

5. Audience Feedback: Adapt and Evolve

- Monitor Comments and Analytics: Pay attention to viewer comments, feedback, and engagement metrics. Use this information to adapt your content strategy, addressing audience preferences and improving over time.

- Adapt to Algorithm Changes: Stay informed about YouTube algorithm changes. Adapt your content strategy to align with algorithm updates, ensuring your videos are optimized for maximum visibility.

Creating quality content for YouTube monetization is a dynamic and evolving process. By understanding your audience, staying current with trends, exploring niches strategically, maintaining consistency, and adapting based on feedback, you set the stage for a successful content creation journey.

Remember, the key is not just to produce content for views but to build a loyal audience that actively engages with your videos. Quality content, combined with strategic niche selection, positions your channel for long-term growth and success in the competitive world of YouTube monetization.

- Crafting Engaging Videos

Creating engaging videos is at the core of building a successful YouTube channel. Whether you're aiming for ad revenue or fostering a dedicated community, captivating content is the key to viewer retention and growth. Here's a comprehensive guide on crafting videos that not only capture attention but also keep viewers coming back for more.

1. Hook Your Audience Early: Compelling Introductions

- Strong Openings: Start your videos with a captivating hook. This could be an intriguing question, a compelling statement, or an engaging visual. Capture your audience's interest within the first few seconds.

- Clear Value Proposition: Communicate what viewers can expect from your video. Outline the benefits or information they will gain by watching, setting clear expectations from the outset.

2. Storytelling Techniques: Keep Viewers Invested

- Narrative Flow: Structure your videos with a logical flow. Whether it's a tutorial, vlog, or informational content, create a narrative that guides viewers from the beginning to the end.

- Personal Connection: Share personal stories or experiences related to your content. Creating an emotional connection with your audience enhances engagement and makes your videos memorable.

3. Visual Appeal: Enhance Aesthetics and Production Quality

- Quality Thumbnails: Design visually appealing thumbnails that accurately represent your video content. Thumbnails serve as the first impression and influence click-through rates.

- High-Quality Production: Invest in good video and audio quality. Clear visuals and crisp sound contribute to a professional-looking video that keeps viewers engaged.

4. Interactive Elements: Encourage Participation

- Calls-to-Action (CTAs): Prompt viewers to like, comment, and subscribe. Encourage interaction by asking questions or inviting viewers to share their thoughts in the comments section.

- Engage with Comments: Respond to viewer comments to foster a sense of community. Acknowledging your audience makes them feel valued and encourages further engagement.

5. Keep it Concise: Respect the Viewer's Time

- Brevity Matters: While detailed content is valuable, avoid unnecessary filler. Keep your videos concise and to the point, respecting your viewers' time.

- Editing Techniques: Use effective editing to maintain a brisk pace. Remove unnecessary pauses or repetitive sections to keep the flow dynamic.

6. Use Visual Variety: Retain Viewer Interest

- Mix-Up Visuals: Integrate a variety of shots, graphics, and animations to maintain visual interest. A dynamic presentation style helps retain viewer attention.

- Visual Storytelling: Leverage visuals to complement your narrative. Use images, graphs, or clips that enhance your message and engage 6 learning styles.

Crafting engaging videos is both an art and a science. By mastering the balance between captivating introductions, compelling storytelling, visual appeal, interactive elements, and concise editing, you create a viewing experience that resonates with your audience.

Remember, each video is an opportunity to strengthen your connection with viewers. Approach your content creation with passion, creativity, and a genuine desire to provide value, and your audience will reward you with their time, loyalty, and, ultimately, your desired monetization goals.

- Optimizing Thumbnails and Titles for Clicks

In the vast sea of YouTube content, capturing attention in a split second is paramount. Thumbnails and titles serve as the gateway to your videos, and optimizing them effectively can significantly impact click-through rates and overall engagement.

Here's a comprehensive guide on how to craft compelling thumbnails and titles that entice viewers to click and watch your content.

1. Eye-Catching Thumbnails: The Visual Invitation

- Clarity is Key: Ensure that your thumbnails are clear and easily understandable, even at smaller sizes. Avoid clutter and prioritize a clean design that conveys the essence of your video.

- Contrasting Colors: Use bold and contrasting colors to make your thumbnails stand out. Vibrant colors attract attention but maintain a cohesive color palette to establish a recognizable brand identity.

- Faces and Emotions: Incorporate expressive faces or emotions in your thumbnails. Humans naturally connect with faces, and conveying emotions can intrigue viewers and make them more likely to click.

2. Compelling Titles: The Gateway to Information

- Keyword Optimization: Integrate relevant keywords in your titles to enhance searchability. Consider what users might type when searching for content similar to yours and incorporate those terms naturally.

- Curiosity and Intrigue: Craft titles that spark curiosity or convey a sense of intrigue. Pose questions, use intriguing statements, or hint at the value viewers will gain from watching your video.

- Clear and Concise: Keep titles clear and concise. Aim for brevity while conveying the essence of your content. Avoid misleading titles, as trust is crucial for building a loyal audience.

3. Consistent Branding: Establishing Recognition

- Branding Elements: Maintain consistent branding elements in your thumbnails, such as logos or a specific font style. This consistency helps viewers instantly recognize your content amidst others.

- Style Guidelines: Establish style guidelines for your thumbnails and titles. Consistency in design enhances the professionalism of your channel and builds a visual identity.

4. Test and Iterate: Analyzing Performance

- A/B Testing: Experiment with different thumbnails and title variations. A/B testing involves creating multiple versions and analyzing their performance to identify what resonates best with your audience.

- Analytics Insights: Leverage YouTube Analytics to track the performance of your thumbnails and titles. Monitor click-through rates (CTR) and adjust your approach based on insights gained from the data.

5. Mobile Optimization: Prioritize Mobile Viewers

- Legibility on Small Screens: Thumbnails and titles should remain legible even on smaller screens. Consider that a significant portion of viewers access YouTube from mobile devices, and your visual elements should cater to this audience.

- High-Impact Design: Optimize your thumbnails for mobile viewing by using high-impact visuals and ensuring that essential information is visible on smaller screens.

Optimizing thumbnails and titles is an ongoing process that requires a balance of creativity and strategic thinking. By creating visually appealing thumbnails, crafting compelling titles, maintaining consistent branding, testing variations, and considering mobile optimization, you enhance your chances of attracting clicks and building a loyal viewership.

Remember, the goal is not just to get clicks but to deliver on the promise made by your thumbnails and titles. Provide valuable content, and your audience will not only click but also stay, engage, and contribute to the success of your YouTube channel.

Chapter 3.

Navigating YouTube's Monetization Policies

- Adherence to Community Guidelines

As a content creator navigating the landscape of YouTube Monetization, understanding and adhering to the platform's policies is essential for long-term success. YouTube's Community Guidelines serve as the cornerstone, outlining the rules and expectations that creators must follow to maintain a monetizable channel. Let's explore the importance of adherence to these guidelines:

1. The Foundation of Monetization: Community Guidelines**

- Content Eligibility: YouTube's Community Guidelines establish the types of content eligible for monetization. To qualify, your content must align with these guidelines, promoting a safe and inclusive environment.

- Quality and Relevance: Adherence to the guidelines ensures that your content maintains a certain standard of quality and relevance. Monetization is not just about quantity but about providing value to viewers in a responsible manner.

2. Prohibited Content: Steering Clear of Red Flags

- Understanding Restrictions: Community Guidelines explicitly state content that is prohibited on the platform. This includes but is not limited to hate speech, violence, nudity, and harmful or dangerous activities.

Familiarize yourself with these restrictions to avoid violations.

- Avoiding Strikes: Violations of Community Guidelines can result in channel strikes. Accumulating multiple strikes can lead to serious consequences, including demonetization or suspension of your channel. Maintaining adherence is crucial to sustaining a monetizable channel.

3. Responsible Monetization: Upholding Ethical Practices

- Advertisement-Friendly Content: Adherence to Community Guidelines ensures your content remains advertisement-friendly. Responsible and ethical content creation is not only essential for maintaining monetization but also for building trust with your audience.

- Viewer Trust and Loyalty: Creators who prioritize adherence to guidelines demonstrate a commitment to creating a positive viewer experience. Viewer trust and loyalty contribute to sustained success on the platform.

4. Reviewing Policies Regularly: Staying Informed

- Policy Updates: YouTube occasionally updates its Community Guidelines. Stay informed about any changes to ensure ongoing compliance. Ignorance of policy updates is not an excuse for violations.

- Creator Updates: YouTube provides regular updates and resources for creators. Regularly check the Creator Insider channel, Help Center, and official communications to stay informed about policy changes and best practices.

5. Content Moderation: A Shared Responsibility

- Community Reporting: YouTube relies on community reporting to identify content that violates guidelines. Encourage your audience to report any content that may breach the guidelines, demonstrating your commitment to a safe and respectful community.

- Moderation Practices: Implement moderation practices for comments on your videos. Addressing inappropriate comments promptly reinforces a positive and respectful environment on your channel.

Navigating YouTube's Monetization Policies begins with a thorough understanding and commitment to upholding the Community Guidelines. Adherenc e not only safeguards your channel's eligibility for monetization but also fosters a healthy and responsible content creation environment.

As you progress on your monetization journey, consider the Community Guidelines as a compass, guiding you towards ethical and successful content creation. Upholding these standards ensures a positive impact not only on your channel's financial aspects but also on the broader YouTube community.

- Copyright and Fair Use

In the dynamic world of YouTube content creation, understanding copyright laws and the concept of fair use is crucial for maintaining a lawful and respectful presence on the platform. Let's delve into the principles of copyright and fair use, outlining guidelines for creators to navigate these creative boundaries responsibly.

1. Copyright Basics: Protecting Creative Works

- Ownership and Rights: Copyright grants creators exclusive rights to their original works, including videos, music, and images. This protection encourages creative expression by safeguarding the economic interests of creators.

- Automatic Protection: Creators don't need to register their works for copyright protection; it is automatic upon creation. This applies to both established creators and those just starting their YouTube journey.

2. Fair Use Doctrine: Balancing Creativity and Copyright

- Legal Exception: Fair use is a legal doctrine that allows limited use of copyrighted material without permission for purposes such as criticism, commentary, news reporting, teaching, scholarship, or research. It serves as a balance between copyright protection and freedom of expression.

- Four Factors: Determining fair use involves considering four factors: the purpose and character of the use, the nature of the copyrighted work, the amount and substantiality of the portion used, and the effect on the market value. No single factor is decisive; they must be considered together.

3. YouTube's Copyright System: Content ID and Claims

- Content ID: YouTube employs Content ID, a system that automatically identifies and manages copyrighted content. This system allows copyright owners to monetize or take down content using their material.

- Handling Claims: If you receive a copyright claim, review the details carefully. Options include acknowledging the claim (if you agree), disputing the claim (if you believe it's invalid), or using YouTube's Audio Library and Creative Commons resources for copyright-free content.

4. Responsible Content Creation: Tips for Creators

- Create Original Content: The surest way to avoid copyright issues is to create original content. Focus on your unique perspective, creativity, and voice to produce videos that stand out.

- Attribution and Permission: When using others' content, provide proper attribution and, when applicable, seek permission. Giving credit is not a substitute for permission, especially if the intended use falls outside fair use.

5. Educate Yourself: Staying Informed on Copyright Laws

- Resources: Familiarize yourself with resources provided by YouTube, such as the Copyright Center and Creator Academy. These platforms offer valuable insights into copyright laws, fair use, and best practices for content creation.

- Legal Consultation: If in doubt, consult with legal professionals specializing in intellectual property or copyright law. Seeking professional advice can help you navigate complex copyright scenarios and make informed decisions.

Copyright and fair use are fundamental aspects of the YouTube ecosystem, shaping how creators share and use content. By understanding copyright basics, embracing the principles of fair use, navigating YouTube's Content ID system responsibly, and staying informed, creators can foster a creative environment that respects intellectual property while expressing unique perspectives. Balancing creativity with legal considerations ensures a thriving and respectful community of content creators on YouTube.

- Avoiding Common Pitfalls

While the prospect of earning revenue on YouTube is exciting, navigating the path to monetization comes with its challenges. Steering clear of common pitfalls is crucial to ensure a smooth and successful journey. Here's a guide to help you avoid the pitfalls that can hinder your progress toward YouTube monetization.

1. Neglecting Quality for Quantity: Content is King

- Quality Over Quantity: Focus on creating high-quality, engaging content rather than churning out a high volume of videos.

Prioritize substance over frequency to build a loyal and engaged audience.

- Rushing the Monetization Process: Don't rush the journey to meet eligibility criteria. Building a solid foundation with quality content and audience engagement takes time, but it sets the stage for long-term success.

2. Ignoring Audience Engagement: The Community Matters

- Neglecting Comments and Feedback: Engage with your audience by responding to comments and feedback. Ignoring your community can lead to a disconnect, hindering the growth of a dedicated viewer base.

- Lack of Consistency: Inconsistency in your upload schedule or content style may confuse your audience. Strive for a consistent approach to build trust and keep viewers coming back.

3. Overlooking Analytics: Data-Driven Insights

- Ignoring YouTube Analytics: Regularly analyze YouTube Analytics to understand your audience's behavior, video performance, and demographics. Insights from analytics help refine your content strategy and optimize for success.

- Not Testing Strategies: A/B tests different thumbnail and title variations, promotional strategies, and content types. Testing allows you to understand what works best for your specific audience.

4. Ignoring SEO Practices: Visibility Matters

- Neglecting Keyword Research: Integrate relevant keywords in titles, descriptions, and tags. Neglecting SEO practices can result in lower discoverability and hinder your potential for increased views.

- Misleading Thumbnails and Titles: Ensure that your thumbnails and titles accurately represent your video content. Misleading practices may result in disappointed viewers and damage your channel's credibility.

5. Impatience and Unrealistic Expectations: The Long Game

- Expecting Immediate Results: YouTube success and monetization often require patience. Building a substantial audience and meeting eligibility criteria take time, so avoid expecting immediate results.

- Setting Unrealistic Goals: Set achievable and realistic goals for your channel's growth. Unrealistic expectations can lead to frustration and may even compromise the quality of your content.

Success on YouTube is a journey marked by strategic decisions, consistent effort, and a deep understanding of your audience. By avoiding common pitfalls such as neglecting content quality, overlooking audience engagement, ignoring analytics, neglecting SEO practices, and maintaining realistic expectations, you pave the way for sustainable growth and success in your YouTube monetization endeavors.

Approach your content creation with a focus on long-term value, and remember that the journey is as important as the destination. By steering clear of these pitfalls, you position yourself for a rewarding and fulfilling experience in the dynamic world of online content creation.

Chapter 4.

Building Your Audience and Increasing Watch Time

- Strategies for Subscriber Growth

Growing your subscriber base on YouTube is a key component of building a successful channel and increasing overall watch time. Here are effective strategies to foster subscriber growth and create a loyal community around your content:

1. Deliver Consistent Value: Content is King

- Quality Content: Prioritize the creation of high-quality, valuable content that resonates with your target audience. A consistent delivery of substance encourages viewers to subscribe for more.

- Educational and Entertaining Mix: Strike a balance between educational and entertaining content. Offering a variety keeps your audience engaged and eager for more.

2. Leverage YouTube Features: Optimize Your Channel

- Customize Channel Layout: Organize your channel layout to highlight your best-performing content. A visually appealing and well-organized channel can attract subscribers.

- Create a Channel Trailer: Craft a compelling channel trailer that succinctly introduces new visitors to the type of content they can expect. A trailer can be a powerful tool for converting viewers into subscribers.

3. Engage with Your Audience: Foster Connection

- Respond to Comments: engage with your audience by responding to comments on your videos. This interaction not only builds a sense of community but also encourages viewers to subscribe.

- Host Q&A Sessions: Periodically host Q&A sessions where you address questions from your audience. This personal touch can strengthen the connection with your viewers.

4. Utilize Social Media: Expand Your Reach

- Promote Your Videos:

Share your videos on various social media platforms to increase visibility. Encourage your social media followers to subscribe to your YouTube channel for more content.

- Leverage Community Features: Utilize community features on YouTube, such as posts and stories, to provide updates and additional content. These features can drive engagement and subscriber growth.

5. Offer Incentives: Entice Subscriptions

- Contests and Giveaways: Host contests or giveaways and require participants to subscribe to your channel. This strategy can attract new subscribers who are interested in your content.

- Exclusive Content for Subscribers: Create special content or perks exclusively for your /. This provides an incentive for viewers to hit the subscribe button.

6. Collaborate with Other Creators: Cross-Promotion

- Collaboration Videos: Partner with other creators in your niche for collaboration videos. Cross-promoting each other exposes your content to new audiences, potentially leading to increased subscribers.

- Participate in Shout-Outs: Participate in shout-out collaborations where you and another creator mutually promote each other's channels. This can be an effective way to expand your subscriber base.

7. Optimize Your Channel Branding: Enhance Recognition

- Eye-Catching Thumbnails and Channel Art: Design visually appealing thumbnails and channel art that create a cohesive and memorable brand. Consistent branding helps in audience recognition.

- Create a Unique Value Proposition: Communicate what sets your channel apart. Establishing a unique value proposition encourages viewers to subscribe to access content they won't find elsewhere.

Subscriber growth is a gradual process that requires dedication and strategic planning. By consistently delivering valuable content, engaging with your audience, leveraging YouTube features, utilizing social media, offering incentives, collaborating with other creators, and optimizing your channel branding, you set the stage for increased subscribers and enhanced watch time.

Remember, the journey to a thriving YouTube channel is dynamic, and success comes not just from numbers but from building a genuine community that values your content. Stay committed to your vision, adapt your strategies based on audience feedback, and enjoy the process of growing and engaging with your subscriber base.

- Enhancing Viewer Engagement

Viewer engagement is the lifeblood of a successful YouTube channel. It goes beyond numbers; it's about building a community that actively interacts with your content. Here's a comprehensive guide on strategies to enhance viewer engagement and foster a strong connection with your audience.

1. Encourage Interaction: Foster a Two-Way Communication

- Ask Questions: Pose questions in your videos to encourage viewers to share their thoughts in the comments. Responding to comments further strengthens the bond between you and your audience.

- Polls and Surveys: Use YouTube's built-in features like polls and community posts to gather feedback and preferences from your audience. This involvement makes video ewers feel valued.

2. Create Compelling Content: Capture and Retain Interest

- Engaging Introductions: Hook your audience right from the beginning. A captivating introduction sets the tone for and encourages viewers to stay engaged.

- Storytelling Techniques: Incorporate storytelling elements in your videos. Narratives create a connection with your audience, making them more invested in your content.

3. Utilize End Screens and Cards: Guide Viewer Journey

- End Screens: Use end screens to direct viewers to other videos or playlists on your channel. This keeps them on your channel longer, contributing to increased watch time and engagement.

- Cards: Integrate cards strategically throughout your videos to suggest related content or prompt viewers to subscribe. These subtle cues guide viewer behavior and enhance engagement.

4. Live Interactions: Real-Time Connection

- Host Live Sessions: Schedule live streams to interact with your audience in real-time. Respond to live comments, answer questions, and create a sense of immediacy that fosters community.

- Q&A Sessions: Periodically host Q&A sessions, where you address questions from your audience. This personal touch adds authenticity and builds a stronger connection.

5. Community Features: Utilize YouTube's Tools

- Community Posts: Use the community tab to share updates, behind-the-scenes content, or additional insights. This feature allows for regular interaction with your audience outside of video uploads.

- Premieres: Premiere new videos and watch them with your audience in real time. The live chat during premieres creates a shared viewing experience and boosts engagement.

6. Social Media Engagement: Extend Your Reach

- Promote on Social Platforms: Share your videos on various social media platforms. Encourage your followers to engage with your content and subscribe to your channel.

- Respond to Mentions: Monitor social media for mentions of your content. Responding to mentions not only acknowledges your audience but also encourages further interaction.

7. Host Contests and Challenges: Spark Participation

- Contests: Host contests or giveaways that require viewers to engage with your content, subscribe, or share. Contests can generate excitement and increase overall engagement.

- Challenge Participation: Create challenges related to your niche and encourage viewers to participate. This involvement not only boosts engagement but also expands your content's reach.

8. Analyze Audience Insights: Adapt and Optimize

- YouTube Analytics: Regularly analyze audience insights to understand viewer demographics, watch time patterns, and popular content. Use this data to tailor your content strategy for maximum engagement.

- A/B Testing: Experiment with different thumbnail and title variations, content styles, and posting schedules. A/B testing helps identify what resonates best with your audience.

Enhancing viewer engagement is a dynamic process that requires ongoing effort and adaptability. By encouraging interaction, creating compelling content, utilizing YouTube features, hosting live sessions, engaging on social media, and analyzing audience insights, you lay the foundation for a thriving YouTube community.

Remember, a dedicated and engaged audience is more likely to contribute to increased watch time, higher visibility, and, ultimately, success in your YouTube monetization journey. Stay connected with your audience, listen to their feedback, and enjoy the collaborative experience of building a vibrant YouTube community.

- Maximizing Watch Time through Playlists and Series

Watch time is a critical factor for YouTube monetization, and leveraging playlists and series is a powerful strategy to maximize viewer engagement and extend watch sessions. Here's a comprehensive guide on how to strategically use playlists and series to enhance watch time on your YouTube channel.

1. The Power of Playlists: Curate Cohesive Content

- Thematic Playlists: Group related videos into thematic playlists. This encourages viewers to watch multiple videos consecutively, contributing to extended watch time.

- Create a Playlist Schedule: Plan and release playlists strategically. Consider creating playlists for specific days or themes to build anticipation and encourage viewers to explore your content further.

2. Structured Series: Guiding Viewer Journey

- Create Engaging Series: Develop a series with consistent themes or storylines. A structured series not only captures viewers ' interest but also encourages them to follow the progression of episodes.

- Introductory and Recap Videos: Include introductory videos for each series to attract new viewers. Recap videos before the start of a new episode refresh viewers' memories, promoting continued engagement.

3. Utilize End Screens: Seamless Video Transition

- End Screen Promotions: Use end screens to promote the next video in a series or suggest another relevant playlist. This seamless transition encourages viewers to keep watching.

- Playlist End Screens: Include playlist end screens to guide viewers to the next set of videos. This feature keeps them immersed in your content, leading to longer watch sessions.

4. Strategic Video Order: Optimize Playlist Flow

- Arrange Videos Thoughtfully: Arrange videos within playlists strategically. Place more engaging or crucial videos earlier in the playlist to capture viewers' attention from the start.

- Variety in Video Lengths: Mix video lengths within a playlist. Combining shorter and longer videos caters to different viewer preferences and keeps the viewing experience dynamic.

5. Consistent Thumbnails and Titles: Visual Cohesion

- Branded Thumbnails: Maintain a consistent thumbnail style for videos within a series or playlist. Branded thumbnails create visual cohesion and help viewers identify related content.

- Coordinated Titles: Use coordinated titles that indicate the video's position in a series or playlist. Clear, sequential titles guide viewers through the content journey and entice them to watch more.

6. Encourage Binge-Watching: Auto-play and Recommendations

- Auto-play Feature: Enable the auto-play feature for playlists. This feature automatically starts the next video, encouraging viewers to continue watching without interruptions.

- Strategic Recommendations: Optimize your video descriptions to include links to other relevant playlists or series. Encourage viewers to explore additional content beyond the current video.

7. Monitor Analytics: Refine and Optimize

- Playlist Analytics: Regularly analyze playlist analytics to understand viewer behavior. Identify which playlists are performing well and refine your strategy based on insights.

- Adapt Based on Trends: Pay attention to viewer trends within playlists and series. Adapt your content strategy based on popular themes or video types to maximize watch time.

Strategically utilizing playlists and series is a dynamic way to boost watch time on your YouTube channel. By curating cohesive playlists, creating engaging series, optimizing video order, and encouraging binge-watching, you enhance the viewer experience and increase the likelihood of reaching YouTube's monetization thresholds.

Remember, the goal is not just to accumulate watch time but to provide a satisfying viewing journey for your audience. Continuously monitor analytics, adapt based on viewer behavior, and enjoy the process of building a channel that keeps viewers engaged and coming back for more.

Chapter 5.

Exploring Different Monetization Channels

- Ad Revenue and Google AdSense

Monetizing your content on YouTube opens the door to various revenue streams, and one of the primary channels is ad revenue, facilitated by Google AdSense. Understanding how ad revenue works and optimizing your strategy can significantly impact your earnings. Here's a comprehensive guide to delve into this monetization channel.

Ad Revenue on YouTube: A Core Monetization Stream

Ad revenue is generated when advertisements are displayed alongside or within your YouTube videos. YouTube partners with Google AdSense to facilitate this process. Here's how it works:

1. Join the YouTube Partner Program (YPP): To be eligible for ad revenue, you need to meet YouTube's criteria for the YouTube Partner Program. This includes having more than 1,000 subscribers, 4,000 watch hours in the past 12 months, and adhering to YouTube's policies.

2. Enable Monetization on Your Channel: Once accepted into YPP, you can enable monetization on your videos. This allows YouTube to display ads before, during, or after your content.

3. Google AdSense Integration: Ad revenue is processed through Google AdSense, Google's advertising platform. You need to link your YouTube account to an AdSense account to receive payments.

4. Ad Formats: Various ad formats are contributing to ad revenue:
   - Pre-roll Ads: Displayed before your video starts.
   - Mid-roll Ads: Appearing during longer videos.
   - Post-roll Ads: Shown at the end of your video.

Optimizing Ad Revenue Strategy: Best Practices

1. Audience Retention:
Longer watch times lead to more ad impressions and increased revenue. Focus on creating engaging content that keeps viewers watching.

2. Strategic Ad Placement: Experiment with different ad placements. While too many ads may deter viewers, strategic placement can optimize revenue without compromising user experience.

3. Diversify Content Types: Diversify your content to attract a broader audience. This can lead to increased views and, consequently, higher ad revenue.

4. Promote Your Videos: Actively promote your videos to increase views. More views mean more opportunities for ad impressions and revenue.

5. Consistent Upload Schedule: A consistent upload schedule can contribute to increased watch time and, subsequently, higher ad revenue. Regular content keeps your audience engaged.

6. Engage with Your Community: Building an engaged community encourages viewers

to watch more of your content, contributing to increased ad revenue. Respond to comments and foster a sense of community.

Google AdSense: The Financial Link

Google AdSense is the financial backbone of YouTube ad revenue. Here's an overview:

1. AdSense Approval: Your AdSense account needs to be approved before you can start earning. Google reviews your content, ensuring it complies with their policies.

2. Payment Threshold: Google AdSense has a payment threshold that you must reach before receiving payouts. Ensure you've set up your payment details correctly in AdSense.

3. AdSense Revenue Sources: Beyond YouTube, you can use AdSense on other

online platforms, such as websites or blogs, to maximize your revenue potential.

Ad revenue, facilitated through Google AdSense, is a foundational monetization channel on YouTube. By understanding the YouTube Partner Program, optimizing your content for engagement, and effectively integrating AdSense, you pave the way for sustainable earnings.

Remember, while ad revenue is a significant channel, exploring additional revenue streams such as merchandise, memberships, or sponsored content can further diversify your income sources. Continuously refine your strategies, stay updated with YouTube policies, and enjoy the journey of building a lucrative and rewarding channel.

- Channel Memberships and Super Chat

In the dynamic world of content creation on YouTube, creators have access to innovative features like Channel Memberships and Super Chat, providing exciting avenues for both engagement and monetization. Let's explore how these features can enhance your connection with your audience and contribute to your channel's financial success.

Channel Memberships: Exclusive Community Engagement

Channel Memberships allow creators to establish a membership program on their channel, providing exclusive perks to paying members. Here's how you can leverage this feature:

1. Eligibility and Activation:

- To activate Channel Memberships, your channel must be part of the YouTube Partner Program. Once eligible, you can set up various membership tiers, each offering unique benefits.

2. Member-Only Content:
    - Create special content exclusively for channel members. This could include behind-the-scenes footage, early access to videos, or personalized messages. Providing exclusive content encourages viewers to become members.

3. Custom Badges and Emojis:
    - Reward your members with custom badges and emojis. These visual identifiers showcase their loyalty in comments and live chats, fostering a sense of community and recognition.

4. Members-Only Community:
    - Establish a dedicated community space for your members. This could be a

members-only Discord server or a community tab on YouTube. Engaging with your members in an exclusive environment strengthens the bond between you and your most dedicated fans.

5. Regular Recognition:
    - Acknowledge and appreciate your members regularly. Whether it's in the credits of your videos or during live streams, recognizing your members reinforces their importance and encourages others to join.

Super Chat: Amplifying Live Stream Interactivity

Super Chat is a feature designed to enhance livestream interactions by allowing viewers to make monetary contributions to highlight their messages. Here's how to maximize the potential of Super Chat:

1. Activation and Monetization:

- Ensure your channel is monetized and live streaming is enabled. Once activated, Super Chat becomes available during your live streams.

2. Viewer Contributions:
   - Viewers can purchase Super Chats of different values to make their messages stand out during live chats. The color and duration of the Super Chat depend on the amount paid.

3. Acknowledgment and Interaction:
   - Acknowledge Super Chat contributions during your live streams. Responding to Super Chats not only expresses gratitude but also makes viewers feel more involved in the live-stream experience.

4. Setting Guidelines:
   - Communicate any guidelines or rules related to Super Chats. Maintaining a positive and respectful environment is

crucial, and setting expectations ensures a smooth livestream experience.

5. Interactive Challenges and Q&A:
   - Use Super Chat to spark interactive challenges or Q&A sessions during live streams. Encourage viewers to participate and contribute to the conversation, creating a dynamic and engaging live stream.

Optimizing Your Monetization Strategy: A Balanced Approach

1. Diversify Revenue Streams:
   - While Channel Memberships and Super Chat are valuable, consider diversifying your income sources. Explore merchandise sales, affiliate marketing, and sponsored content to create a well-rounded monetization strategy.

2. Communicate the Value:
   - Communicate the value of Channel Memberships and Super Chat to your

audience. Highlight the exclusive perks, engagement opportunities, and the impact their support has on the growth of your channel.

3. Promote and Integrate:
  - Actively promote Channel Memberships and supercars during your content and live streams. Integration of these features should feel seamless, and your audience should be aware of the benefits of becoming a member or participating in Super Chats.

4. Listen and Adapt:
  - Regularly gather feedback from your audience regarding Channel Memberships and Super Chat. Adapt your approach based on their preferences, ensuring that the features align with the evolving expectations of your community.

Channel Memberships and Super Chat empower creators to build stronger connections with their audience while providing additional avenues for revenue. By implementing these features strategically, creators can enhance their monetization strategy, deepen community engagement, and create a more sustainable and rewarding YouTube experience. Stay attuned to your audience's needs, experiment with new ideas, and relish the journey of fostering a vibrant and supportive community on your channel.

- Sponsored Content and Affiliate Marketing

In the ever-evolving landscape of YouTube monetization, creators have the opportunity to diversify their income through sponsored content and affiliate marketing. These avenues not only provide additional revenue streams but also enable creators to collaborate with brands and promote products they genuinely believe in. Here's a guide on effectively incorporating sponsored content and affiliate marketing into your YouTube strategy.

Sponsored Content: A Collaborative Partnership

Sponsored content involves collaborating with brands or companies to create content that promotes their products or services. Here's how to make the most of sponsored collaborations:

1. Authenticity is Key:
   - Choose sponsorships that align with your channel's niche and values. Authenticity fosters trust with your audience, and promoting products you genuinely believe in enhances your credibility.

2. Disclose and Be Transparent:

- Always disclose sponsored content to your audience. Transparency builds trust, and being upfront about sponsored collaborations ensures an open and honest relationship with your viewers.

3. Create Engaging Content:
- Craft sponsored content that seamlessly integrates into your usual content style. Engaging storytelling and a natural presentation make sponsored videos more enjoyable for your audience.

4. Highlight Benefits:
- Communicate the benefits of the sponsored product or service. Showcase how it adds value to your audience's lives, making them more likely to consider or try the promoted item.

5. Collaborate with Relevance:
- Seek partnerships that resonate with your audience. Collaborating with brands relevant to your content enhances the

viewer experience and increases the likelihood of positive reception.

Affiliate Marketing: Earning Through Recommendations

Affiliate marketing involves promoting products or services through unique affiliate links, earning a commission for each sale or action generated through those links. Here's how to effectively incorporate affiliate marketing into your content:

1. Select Relevant Affiliates:
   - Choose affiliate programs and products that align with your content and audience interests. Promoting relevant products enhances the likelihood of conversions.

2. Transparent Disclosures:
   - Disclose your use of affiliate links in your content. Honesty builds trust, and transparent communication ensures your

audience is aware of any potential affiliate relationships.

3. Create Compelling Content:

- Integrate affiliate promotions naturally into your content. Develop engaging narratives or demonstrations that showcase the benefits of the product or service.

4. Educate and Add Value:

- Provide valuable information about the promoted products. Educate your audience on how these products can solve problems or enhance their lives, making your recommendations more compelling.

5. Strategic Placement:

- Strategically place affiliate links in your video descriptions or accompanying content. Make it easy for your audience to find and use the links if they are interested in the promoted products.

Optimizing Your Approach: A Harmonious Blend

1. Balancing Sponsored and Regular Content:
   - Maintain a balance between sponsored and regular content. Overloading your channel with sponsored material can dilute authenticity, while occasional, well-integrated promotions can enhance viewer interest.

2. Research and Negotiation:
   - Research potential sponsors and affiliate programs thoroughly. Negotiate terms that align with your values and provide fair compensation for your efforts.

3. Measure Performance:
   - Regularly analyze the performance of sponsored content and affiliate links. Understand what resonates with your audience and refine your approach based on the insights gathered.

4. Stay True to Your Brand:
    - Prioritize authenticity in all your collaborations. Stay true to your brand identity, and choose sponsorships and affiliates that align with your values and the expectations of your audience.

Sponsored content and affiliate marketing offer creators the opportunity to diversify their revenue streams while providing valuable content to their audience. By maintaining authenticity, transparency, and relevance in collaborations, creators can strike a harmonious balance between monetization and audience satisfaction. Continuously adapt your approach, listen to your audience's feedback, and enjoy the process of building a sustainable and rewarding content creation journey on YouTube.

Chapter 6

Analyzing Performance and Scaling Revenue

- Utilizing YouTube Analytics

As a content creator on YouTube, understanding your channel's performance is crucial for both growth and revenue scaling. YouTube Analytics provides a wealth of data and insights that can guide your strategic decisions. Let's explore how to effectively utilize YouTube Analytics to analyze performance and scale your revenue.

Unlocking YouTube Analytics: An Overview

1. Accessing YouTube Analytics:

- Navigate to your YouTube Studio dashboard and select "Analytics." Here, you'll find a comprehensive overview of your channel's performance.

2. Key Metrics:
- Watch Time: A critical metric for monetization, watch time reflects the total minutes viewers spend watching your content.
- Views and Click-Through Rate (CTR): Monitor the number of views and CTR to understand how effectively your thumbnails and titles attract clicks.
- Revenue and RPM (Revenue per Mille): Track your earnings and RPM, which indicates the revenue you earn per thousand impressions.

Optimizing Content Strategy: Insights from Analytics

1. Top-Performing Videos:

- Identify your top-performing videos in terms of watch time and views. Analyze what makes these videos successful and consider creating more content in a similar vein.

2. Audience Demographics:
- Explore the demographic data of your audience. Understanding the age, gender, and location of your viewers helps tailor content that resonates with your core audience.

3. Traffic Sources:
- Examine where your traffic is coming from—whether it's from YouTube searches, external websites, or other sources. Optimize your content to capitalize on high-performing traffic sources.

4. Engagement Metrics:
- Assess engagement metrics like likes, comments, and shares. High engagement indicates content resonating with your

audience, contributing positively to revenue potential.

Monetization Insights: Revenue and RPM

1. Revenue Overview:
   - Track your revenue over time. Identify trends and correlate them with specific content or promotional strategies.

2. RPM Analysis:
   - Evaluate your RPM to understand how effectively you're converting views into revenue. Higher RPMs often indicate optimized monetization strategies.

3. Top-Earning Videos:
   - Identify your top-earning videos and analyze commonalities. Replicate successful elements in future content to boost overall revenue.

Scaling Revenue: Strategic Action Steps

1. Content Iteration;
    - Iterate your content based on the insights gained. Focus on creating content that aligns with audience preferences, resulting in increased watch time and, consequently, higher revenue.

2. Audience Expansion:
    - Leverage demographic data to tailor content for a broader audience. Expanding your viewer base can lead to increased views and, subsequently, higher revenue potential.

3. Optimized Thumbnails and Titles:
    - Use CTR data to refine your thumbnail and title strategies. A higher CTR can lead to increased views, positively impacting both watch time and revenue.

4. Promotional Strategies:
    - Experiment with different promotional strategies, including sponsored content, affiliate marketing, and collaborations.

Analyze the performance of these strategies and refine your approach for maximum revenue impact.

5. Consistent Engagement:
   - Maintain consistent engagement with your audience. Respond to comments, conduct polls, and host live sessions. An engaged audience is more likely to contribute to increased watch time and revenue.

YouTube Analytics is a powerful tool that empowers creators to make data-driven decisions for optimizing performance and scaling revenue. By leveraging insights from top-performing videos, audience demographics, engagement metrics, and revenue analytics, creators can refine their content strategy and monetization approaches. Regularly analyze your YouTube Analytics, adapt your strategies based on the data, and enjoy the journey of building a successful and sustainable YouTube channel.

- Iterative Improvement of Content and Strategy

In the dynamic landscape of content creation on YouTube, the journey toward success is marked by continuous evolution and refinement. Iterative improvement of your content and strategy is not just a necessity; it's the key to staying relevant, engaging your audience, and achieving sustained growth. Let's delve into the principles and practices that make up this blueprint for success.

1. Embrace the Analytical Mindset: YouTube Analytics as Your Guide

1.1 Regular Data Review:

- Make a habit of regularly reviewing your YouTube Analytics. Understand what's working well—examining metrics like watch time, click-through rate (CTR), and audience demographics.

1.2 Identify Trends and Patterns:
- Look for trends and patterns in your data. Recognize the types of content that resonate most with your audience and leverage this knowledge in shaping your content strategy.

1.3 Performance Benchmarking:
- Establish benchmarks for key metrics. Compare the performance of new videos against these benchmarks to assess growth and identify areas for improvement.

2. Engage with Your Community: The Heartbeat of Your Channel

2.1 Listen to Feedback:

- Actively listen to audience feedback through comments, polls, and community posts. Understand what your viewers appreciate and what improvements they suggest.

2.2 Community Interaction:
- Foster community engagement by responding to comments, asking questions, and involving your audience in decisions. A strong sense of community encourages viewer loyalty.

2.3 Iterative Content Based on Feedback:
- Iterate your content based on audience feedback. If certain topics or styles resonate more, incorporate them into your content plan for continuous improvement.

3. Evolution of Content Quality: From Good to Exceptional

3.1 Production Quality Enhancement:

- Gradually enhance the production quality of your videos. Invest in better equipment, refine your editing skills, and explore creative ways to make your content visually appealing.

3.2 Content Structure Refinement:
- Refine the structure of your content. Pay attention to pacing, storytelling, and the overall flow of your videos. A well-structured video keeps viewers engaged from start to finish.

3.3 Diversification of Content Types
- Experiment with different content types. Introduce variety in your content to cater to different audience preferences and keep your channel dynamic and interesting.

4. Consistent Branding: Creating a Cohesive Channel Identity

4.1 Visual Branding Elements:

- Establish consistent visual elements across your channel, such as thumbnails, channel art, and logos. Recognizable branding fosters a sense of identity and trust among your audience.

4.2 Tone and Messaging Consistency:
- Maintain a consistent tone and messaging in your videos. Whether your style is informative, entertaining, or a blend, coherence builds a stronger connection with your audience.

4.3 Channel Value Proposition:
- Communicate your channel's value proposition. Help viewers understand what makes your content unique and why they should subscribe and engage with your channel.

5. Experimentation and Adaptability: Key Components of Growth

5.1 Content Experimentation:

- Be willing to experiment with new content ideas. Some experiments may not yield the expected results, but each provides valuable insights that contribute to your channel's evolution.

5.2 Adaptation to Trends:
- Stay updated with industry trends and changes in viewer behavior. Adapt your content and strategy to align with these trends, ensuring your channel remains relevant and appealing.

5.3 Flexibility in Monetization Strategies:
- Be flexible in your approach to monetization. Explore various revenue streams, adapt your strategies based on performance, and embrace opportunities that align with your brand.

6. Learning from Challenges: Turning Setbacks into Progressï

6.1 Analyzing Setbacks:

- Analyze setbacks objectively. Understand the reasons behind video underperformance or shifts in audience engagement. Use setbacks as learning opportunities for improvement.

6.2 Course Correction:
- Implement course corrections based on lessons learned. Adjust your content strategy, engagement approach, or production techniques to overcome challenges and steadily progress.

6.3 Resilience and Persistence:
- Cultivate resilience and persistence. Challenges are inherent in any creative journey, and overcoming them contributes to your growth as a creator.

The iterative improvement of content and strategy is a perpetual cycle—one that involves learning, adapting, experimenting, and evolving. Embrace each phase of the journey with enthusiasm, use data-driven insights as your guide, and never underestimate the power of consistent, thoughtful improvement. By embodying this mindset, you not only build a successful YouTube channel but also establish a foundation for enduring creativity and audience connection.

- Scaling Monetization Efforts Beyond YouTube

Scaling Monetization Efforts Beyond YouTube opens up new avenues for content creators to diversify their income streams and reach a broader audience. Here's a glimpse into the strategies and opportunities available:

1. Leveraging Other Platforms:

- Expand your content to platforms like Twitch, Instagram, or TikTok.
- Tailor content to each platform's audience while maintaining your unique style.

2. Podcasting and Audio Monetization:
- Convert your expertise into podcasts for platforms like Spotify or Apple Podcasts.
- Explore sponsorship and advertising opportunities within the podcasting space.

3. Online Courses and Educational Content:
- Develop in-depth courses on platforms like Udemy or Teachable.
- Monetize your expertise by offering exclusive educational content.

4. Merchandise and Brand Collaborations:
- Design and sell branded merchandise through platforms like Teespring.
- Partner with brands for collaborations, extending your reach beyond video content.

5. Affiliate Marketing Beyond YouTube:

- Integrate affiliate links into blog posts, newsletters, or social media.

- Explore niche websites and forums where your audience might be engaged.

6. Membership Platforms and Exclusive Content:

- Utilize Patreon or other membership platforms to offer exclusive perks.

- Create a sense of community with loyal supporters.

7. Live Events and Workshops:

- Host live events or workshops on platforms like Zoom.

- Charge admission or offer premium access for exclusive sessions.

8. E-books and Digital Products:

- Write e-books related to your niche and sell them on platforms like Amazon Kindle.

- Offer downloadable resources, such as templates or guides.

9. Email Marketing Campaigns:
- Build an email list for direct communication with your audience.
- Promote products, courses, or exclusive content through targeted campaigns.

10. Consulting or Coaching Services:
- Offer one-on-one consulting or coaching sessions based on your expertise.
- Use platforms like Clarity.fm to connect with individuals seeking guidance.

11. Webinars and Virtual Summits:
- Host webinars or virtual summits on topics within your niche.
- Monetize through ticket sales, sponsorships, or exclusive access fees.

Scaling monetization efforts beyond YouTube requires a strategic approach and a deep understanding of your audience's preferences. By diversifying your revenue streams, you not only increase your financial stability but also establish a more robust and resilient online presence.

Conclusion

- Recap of Key Strategies

In conclusion, "YouTube Monetization Simplified" equips content creators with essential strategies to navigate the dynamic landscape of online video monetization. Let's recap some key strategies highlighted in this book:

1. Content Quality Is Paramount:
   - Prioritize creating high-quality, engaging content that resonates with your target audience.

2. Audience Building and Engagement:

- Foster a loyal audience by employing strategies for subscriber growth and maximizing viewer engagement.

3. Navigating YouTube's Policies:
- Understand and adhere to YouTube's community guidelines, copyright policies, and avoid common pitfalls that may hinder monetization.

4. Diversify Monetization Channels:
- Explore various revenue streams, including ad revenue, channel memberships, sponsored content, and affiliate marketing.

5. Optimizing for Watch Time and Clicks:
- Strategically use playlists, series, thumbnails, and titles to boost watch time and click-through rates.

6. Scaling Beyond YouTube:

- Expand your reach by leveraging other platforms, exploring podcasting, online courses, merchandise, and collaborations.

7. Analyzing Performance:
   - Utilize YouTube Analytics to continuously evaluate the performance of your videos and refine your content strategy.

8. Building a Sustainable Business Model:
   - Consider long-term sustainability by diversifying income through memberships, e-books, consulting, and live events.

9. Adaptability to Future Trends:
   - Stay informed about evolving trends in the YouTube and online content space to remain relevant and capitalize on emerging opportunities.

In essence, success in YouTube monetization lies in the fusion of creativity, strategic thinking, and adaptability. By incorporating these key strategies, content creators can not only achieve monetization goals on YouTube but also build a robust and sustainable online presence. As the digital landscape evolves, the principles outlined in this book will empower creators to navigate new challenges and seize future opportunities. May your journey towards monetization be simplified and prosperous.

- Future Trends in YouTube Monetization

As technology and consumer behaviors continue to evolve, the future of YouTube monetization is poised for exciting transformations. Content creators should stay ahead of the curve by anticipating and adapting to these emerging trends:

1. Interactive and Immersive Content:

- Embrace interactive content formats, such as shoppable videos or interactive storytelling, to enhance viewer engagement.

2. Virtual and Augmented Reality Monetization:
- Explore opportunities within virtual and augmented reality, allowing for immersive experiences and new monetization avenues.

3. Blockchain and Cryptocurrency Integration:
- Investigate blockchain technology for transparent revenue distribution, and explore cryptocurrencies for transactions within the YouTube ecosystem.

4. Personalized and AI-Driven Content:
- Leverage artificial intelligence to personalize content recommendations, increasing viewer satisfaction and potentially attracting more advertisers.

5.   Niche   Communities   and Micro-Influencers:
   - Capitalize on the rise of niche communities, as advertisers increasingly seek authentic connections with engaged audiences, even on a smaller scale.

6. Livestream Monetization Innovation:
   - Expect continuous innovation in livestream monetization, with new features and tools allowing creators to earn revenue in real-time during broadcasts.

7. Subscription and Premium Models:
   - Explore premium content models or exclusive subscription-based offerings, providing additional value to dedicated audiences.

8. Short-Form Video Monetization:
   - As short-form video gains popularity, creators can monetize through concise, attention-grabbing content and sponsored partnerships.

9. Cross-Platform Monetization Strategies:

- Develop cross-platform strategies, where creators seamlessly monetize content across various platforms, diversifying revenue streams.

10. Ephemeral Content and Story Monetization:

- Embrace the trend of ephemeral content and monetize through sponsored stories, opening up new opportunities for partnerships.

11. Sustainable and Socially Responsible Monetization:

- Emphasize sustainability and social responsibility, as audiences increasingly value creators who align with ethical practices and causes.

12. Integrated Shopping and E-Commerce:

- Explore integrated shopping experiences within YouTube, allowing creators to monetize through product placements and direct e-commerce partnerships.

In navigating the future of YouTube monetization, content creators should remain agile, adaptive, and open to experimenting with emerging trends. The intersection of technology, creativity, and business acumen will be crucial in unlocking the full potential of monetization on YouTube and beyond. By staying informed and embracing innovation, creators can position themselves for sustained success in an ever-evolving digital landscape.

www.ingramcontent.com/pod-product-compliance
Lightning Source LLC
Chambersburg PA
CBHW071208290526
45796CB00008B/180